T0193453

Grammy and Papa's
Big Back Yard

Jeannette Hollowell

Archway Publishing books may be ordered through booksellers or by contacting:

Archway Publishing
1663 Liberty Drive
Bloomington, IN 47403
www.archwaypublishing.com
844-669-3957

Interior Image Credit: Marta Maszkiewicz

ISBN: 978-1-6657-2888-1 (sc)
ISBN: 978-1-6657-2939-0 (hc)
ISBN: 978-1-6657-2887-4 (e)

Print information available on the last page.

Archway Publishing rev. date: 9/22/2022

About the Author

. . . .

Jeannette loves to observe nature. The addition of a back yard pond, built by her husband, brought new sights and sounds, and her love for writing poetry took flight. She lives in Virginia and taught young children for many years. This is her first book.

Grammy and Papa's Big Back Yard

In Grammy and Papa's big back yard,
having fun is never hard.

Many animals can be found.
They fly and swim and scamper around.

Let's take a look, just you and me.

Open your eyes.
What do you see?

1
One

One baby bunny nibbling the flowers.
She looks like she could eat
for hours and hours.

2
Two

Two tiny hummingbirds
with beaks so long
fly quickly by while
singing their song.

3
Three

Three baby bluebirds
chirping up a storm,
snuggled in their nest where
mom keeps them warm.

4
Four

Four gray squirrels playing
tag in the trees,
running from limb to limb
and jumping with ease.

5
Five

Five big bullfrogs on the rocks in the pond,
waiting for insects of which they are fond.

6
Six

Six hungry birds perched
on the feeders.
Every morning and evening,
they are such big eaters.

7
Seven

Seven orange fish in the
pond so bright;
the grandchildren grin and
are filled with delight.

8
Eight

Eight colorful dragonflies
without a care,
searching for insects while
flying through the air.

9
Nine

Nine fancy monarchs with
wings orange and black,
landing on flowers and
finding a snack.

10
Ten

Ten busy honeybees fly out of the hive,

leaving friends by the thousands

working inside.

From your visit today,

I hope you will agree,

Grammy and Papa's yard

is a fun place to be.

Printed in the United States
by Baker & Taylor Publisher Services